'This pamphlet sets the record straight. It stands with the victims of imperialism and war – with the workers and peasants of Europe, and with the colonial people of Africa and Asia. It argues that the Somme, by any rational assessment, represents a world gone mad.'

Have you forgotten yet?
THE TRUTH ABOUT THE SOMME
by
Neil Faulkner

Dr Neil Faulkner is a leading First World War archaeologist and a research fellow at Bristol University. He co-directs field projects in Britain, Jordan, and Slovenia. He works as a lecturer, writer, editor, and broadcaster. His latest book is *Lawrence of Arabia's War: The Arabs, The British and the Remaking of the Middle East in WW1*.

No Glory is a campaign committed to challenging any attempts to sanitise, excuse or glorify the global conflict that took place between 1914 and 1918. Look out for our 2014 pamphlet *No Glory: the real history of the First World War* by Neil Faulkner.
www.noglory.org

Edited by Jan Woolf
Design and layout by Matthew Crampton
The phrase 'Have you forgotten yet?' comes from the poem Aftermath by Siegfried Sassoon.
Front cover: *Box Wallah*, fragment, by Steve Hurst; back cover: *Box Wallah*, by Steve Hurst; photography by Steve Russell.
Photos on page 26 courtesy of Imperial War Museum: Q33007, Q3934 and Q1471. Other illustrations from private collection.

First edition May 2016
ISBN 978-0-9561361-3-8
© No Glory in War 2016

CONTENTS

INTRODUCTION   4
Soldiers
Historians

1. STALEMATE   8
'To the last million'
Storm of steel
Attrition

2. BLOOD MILL   15
'At a steady pace'
'A muddy grave?'

3. A WAR FOR EMPIRE AND PROFIT   22
Anglo-German rivalry
A systemic crisis
From war to revolution

DANDELIONS   30
A song by Steve O'Donoghue

HARRY PATCH   32

If you want to find the General

INTRODUCTION

The Somme was Britain's bloodiest battle. It lasted almost five months, from late June to mid November 1916, and cost more than a million casualties, about 40% of them British.

Many of the latter were 'New Army' men – volunteers who had joined up since the start of the war. Many had joined 'pals' battalions' formed of friends from the same factories and neighbourhoods.

Sometimes, when a pals' battalion went into action on the Somme, almost everyone was killed or wounded. When this happened, the local paper back home would list the hundreds of names, and an entire town would be plunged into grief.

None of it made any difference. The front-line advanced a few miles, but the Germans remained as strongly entrenched as ever, and the war continued for another two years.

Soldiers

The Somme has been a symbol of slaughter and stalemate – and therefore of the waste and futility of war – for a century. The revulsion started in the trenches, among the men who fought the battle. Men like war-poet Siegfried Sassoon.

Moving down a long communication trench with his battalion, Sassoon passed

> ... three very mangled corpses lying in it: a man, short, plump, with turned-up moustache, lying face downward and half sideways with one arm flung up as if defending his head, and a bullet through his forehead. A doll-like figure. Another hunched

I know where he is

and mangled, twisted and scorched with many days' dark
growth on his face, teeth clenched and grinning lips.

Images of the dead on the Somme lodged in his mind and destroyed his support for the war. Death, which the year before had been 'noble', became 'horrible'. The prospect of victory was now 'more terrible than defeat'.

Writing in his diary after the battle, he quoted Mr Britling, the main character in a new novel by H G Wells:

> It is a war without point, a war that has lost its soul; it has become mere incoherent fighting and destruction, a demonstration in vast and tragic forms of the stupidity and ineffectiveness of our species.

Sassoon dreamed of turning his own soldiers against 'the corpse-commanders in red and gold', 'the junkers in Parliament', and 'the yellow-pressmen' who bayed for war.

After the Somme, a gulf separated the soldiers who had served at the front from civilians back home fed on lies. 'England looked strange to us returned soldiers,' wrote Robert Graves, another war-poet who fought on the Somme.

> We could not understand the war-madness that ran wild everywhere, looking for a pseudo-military outlet. The civilians talked a foreign language; and it was newspaper language.

Graves now found himself disgusted by the military:

> *The training principles had recently been revised.* Infantry Training, 1914 *laid it down politely that the soldier's ultimate aim was to put out of action or render ineffective the armed forces of the enemy. The War Office no longer considered this statement direct enough for a war of attrition. Troops learned*

He's pinning another medal on his chest

instead that they must HATE the Germans, and KILL as many of them as possible. In bayonet-practice, the men had to make horrible grimaces and utter blood-curdling yells as they charged. The instructors' faces were set in a permanent ghastly grin. 'Hurt him, now! In at the belly! Tear his guts out!' they would scream as the men charged the dummies.

Historians

A new generation of academics is at work 'revising' the history of the First World War. They tell us that 'the lions led by donkeys' stereotype of British generalship is false; that the British Army learned to fight on the Somme; that the battle was part of a process of attrition to break German resistance; that this was necessary because Germany was a threat to world peace and the balance of power; and also that Germany was an exceptionally aggressive, militaristic, and autocratic imperial power.

This academic revisionism is supported by Tory politicians. They want to use the centenary of the First World War to celebrate 'Britishness' and what they call 'our national spirit'. They want to use Britain's role in the First World War to justify imperialism and war today. The popular view – that the war was a collective human tragedy – must be rejected as naïve and unsophisticated.

The revisionist perspective is deeply flawed. It narrows the view to the machinations of statesmen and the manoeuvres of generals. It ignores the wider context and takes as given a dysfunctional world of competing corporations and rival empires. It accepts uncritically a geopolitical system ruled by bankers, arms manufacturers, and militarists.

This pamphlet sets the record straight. It stands with the

victims of imperialism and war – with the workers and peasants of Europe, and with the colonial people of Africa and Asia. It argues that the Somme, by any rational assessment, represents a world gone mad.

When Alan Clark wrote The Donkeys *in 1961 – portraying Britain's generals as donkeys leading lions – he shattered the nation's deference to the military establishment. The satire* Oh! What A Lovely War *soon followed. Recently, some historians have sought to return to the days when Haig and his chums were treated as heroes.*

Pinning another medal on his chest.

1. STALEMATE

On 1 July 1916, 150,000 British soldiers went 'over the top' to assault the German trench system in the Somme sector of the Western Front. It was the biggest infantry attack in British history.

The German defences on the Somme were made up of consecutive lines of trenches, emplacements, and dug-outs, defended by riflemen, machine-guns, artillery, and barbed wire. The defended zone was thousands of yards deep, so even those who got across no-man's-land into the enemy trenches entered a labyrinth of death.

Most did not get that far. The assault waves were so effectively scythed by machine-guns and blasted by artillery that some battalions lost three-quarters of their men within minutes of leaving their trenches.

Sheltering in a shell-hole near the German wire, Corporal Ashurst looked back across no-man's-land.

> *Hundreds of dead lay about, and wounded men were trying to crawl back to safety. As I lay there watching their painful efforts to get back to our line, I watched these poor fellows suddenly try to rise on their feet and then fall in a heap and lie very still. Shells whistled over my head and dropped among the poor fellows, blowing dead men into the air and putting others out of their agony.*

By the end of the first day of the Somme, 19,000 British soldiers were dead and a further 38,000 wounded. It was the British Empire's bloodiest day. Along most of the front, there had been no gains at all.

'To the last million'

By the time the Somme was fought, the war had lasted almost two years. Most politicians, generals, and journalists had said it would be over in a few months, even weeks. Pre-war planning and mobilisation schedules had assumed so. Railways had made Europe so much smaller. Armies could now be moved from one side of the continent to the other in less than a week. It would be what a later generation would know as *blitzkrieg* – lightning war. Whoever got the most men and guns into action first would win. The outcome would be decided by the railway timetables.

Lord Herbert Kitchener, the British War Minister, was an exception. He said the war would last at least three years, require new mass armies, and cost huge casualties. It would be a war 'to the last million'.

Kitchener knew about modern industrialised warfare. He was a manager of wars of manpower and materiel. He had engineered the mechanised destruction of the Dervishes at the Battle of Omdurman in 1898, a battle of machine-guns against spears, in which the Sudanese lost 25,000 and the British less than 500.

He had orchestrated the defeat of the South African Boers in a two-year counterinsurgency campaign that had involved half a million British soldiers, the construction of 10,000 blockhouses, and the forced removal of 120,000 people into concentration camps where the death-rate soared to one in three.

These had been 'asymmetrical' wars, one against tribesmen with medieval weapons, the other against small numbers of mobile guerrillas. The First World War was the first clash between modern mass armies.

Storm of steel

When it began, in 1914, about 13 million men were mobilised. Before it ended, four years later, more than four times that number had been conscripted.

Even at the outset, these mass armies deployed weapons of unprecedented killing-power. But as war industries ramped up and legions of scientists worked to refine the technology, the firepower became ever more deadly. Between August 1914 and August 1918, the British Army's artillery increased 500%, its machine-guns 3,000%, and its airpower 12,000%. It also created a new tank corps of 30,000 men equipped with a thousand tanks.

What made this possible was the industrialisation of war – the conversion of entire economies to mass production of uniforms, equipment, rations, firearms, artillery, explosives, shells, barbed wire, corrugated iron, trucks, tanks, aircraft, and warships.

It became a war of 'materiel'. Also a war of 'attrition' – a competition to kill and destroy until the opponent was exhausted, drained of manpower, crippled by the cost. A 'total' war in which all economic resources – raw materials, factories, railways, shipping, labour – were mobilised to create killing-power.

The battlefield was transformed. It was no longer a point on the map; it was a line, a 'front'. The Western Front, which stretched from Switzerland to the North Sea, was 440 miles long.

Nor was it a pencil line; it was a thick band, many miles deep. The band was a mesh of trenches and barbed wire, of bunkers, machine-gun nests, and artillery emplacements, all laid across a shell-blasted landscape of mud, stumps, and rubble.

Also a landscape of bodies. Of corpses, and bits of corpses, slowly decomposing, rotting down like compost, gradually turning into earth.

This place – the battle front of the First World War – was like a medieval vision of Hell. But this 12th century vision had been made possible by 20th century technology.

Because the trenches were held by millions of men, and because they deployed firepower of unprecedented ferocity, nothing could get through the 'storm of steel' that dominated no-man's-land.

Rifles had maximum ranges of about 2,000 yards, and a rifleman could fire about ten aimed rounds a minute. Heavy machine-guns, with about twice the range, might take the same time to spray a full belt of 250 rounds across an area 500 yards wide.

Field-guns, with ranges in excess of 6,500 yards, could maintain a steady four rounds a minute. A single shrapnel shell could scatter perhaps 250 high-velocity bullets across 50 yards of 'beaten ground', while high-explosive shells killed by concussion, blast, and the effect of countless flying shards of hot metal.

The achievements of the industrial revolution – the inventions, the machines, the factories, the mass production, the exponential increases in the capacity to satisfy human need – had been transformed into their opposite: a vast mechanism of death, concentrated in thick bands of mud and blood stretched across the European continent. The result was military stalemate.

The politicians demanded results. So many men, so much materiel, such cost, such heaping up of debt: how come, despite all this, no breakthrough? So the generals ordered a succession of frontal attacks. Each failed, and the generals said it was for lack of firepower, and demanded more. So the politicians ramped up the war economy, increasing the flow of men, machines, and munitions into the blood-grinder.

Attrition

It had started as a war of movement. In August 1914, a German Army of a million and a half had swept through Belgium and north-eastern France and almost reached Paris. Then the French counterattacked. The Germans recoiled a little and dug in.

The armies, unable to break through frontally, moved against the flanks. Each time, they were blocked. Each time, both sides dug in. So the trench lines got longer and longer – it became 'a race to the sea' – and by the winter of 1914/15, it was stalemate along the whole of the Western Front.

By then, Britain's first army, the old regular army of long-service professionals, was all used up. So a second army, made up of territorials, part-time reserve soldiers, defended the trenches through 1915.

The British and the French launched a series of attacks on the German lines. These became bigger and bloodier as the year went on. For the British, it culminated in the Battle of Loos.

Fought in the early autumn of 1915 in the bleak landscape of a coalfield, it lasted three weeks and cost 60,000 British casualties. It achieved nothing. The defeat and the carnage caused a political crisis.

The blame for failure fell on the Liberal Government. It was not warlike enough. It was not producing enough shells. It had not introduced conscription. It was not waging what David Lloyd George called 'a holy war' against 'German expansionism'.

Lloyd George was made Minister of Munitions and began constructing a 'total war' economy based on conscription of single men and state-directed arms production.

As early as May 1915, *The Times* – the paper of bankers, industrialists, and war profiteers – had headlined: 'Need for shells: British attacks checked: Limited supply the cause: A lesson

Sitting in comfort, stuffing his bloody gut.

from France'.

> *We had not sufficient high explosives to lower the enemy's parapets to the ground ... The want of an unlimited supply of high explosives was a fatal bar to our success.*

So shell production ramped up, increasing from 500,000 in 1914, to 16 million in 1915, and 50 million in the last year of the war. In all, the British Army would fire 170 million shells during the First World War.

Artillery caused about 70% of the casualties. Sometimes exploding shells blew men apart so comprehensively that they were vapourised, leaving no visible trace. Sometimes they blew bits of them away – limbs, faces, eyes – leaving victims in torments of agony and maimed for life. Sometimes they discharged poison gas and men suffocated as their lungs burnt out.

Ever more of the shells – in Britain and across Europe – were made by women. Millions of working-class women toiling to make weapons to destroy millions of working-class men – and profits for the arms-manufacturers. Such was the madness of the war.

Could it not have been ended? As early as late 1914, with the war in stalemate, Germany's leaders approached the Russians and the French about peace. Diplomatic contacts of one sort or another continued throughout the war.

But they never came to anything. Neither side would give ground while it held the advantage. And in a war, someone always holds the advantage.

The German Kaiser wanted to create a 'Middle Europe' zone dominated by German capitalism – a European empire to rival the African and Asian empires of the British and the French. The Russian Tsar wanted Constantinople and the Caucasus. The British and the French were planning to dismember the

Ottoman Empire and divide the Middle East between them.

For these reasons, regardless of cost, even though the cost exceeded all expectations, the killing went on.

> THE BATTLE OF THE SOMME.   45
>
> at Fricourt had nine rooms and five bolt-holes; it had iron doors, gas curtains, linoleum on the floors, wallpaper and pictures on the walls, and boasted a good bath-room, electric light, and electric bells. The staff which occupied it must have lived in luxury. Many of these dug-outs had two stories, a thirty-foot staircase, beautifully finished, leading to the first suite, and a second stair of the same length conducting to a lower story. In such places machine guns could be protected during any bombardment. But the elaboration of such dwellings went far beyond military needs. When the Germans boasted that their front on the West was impregnable they sincerely believed it. They thought they had established a continuing city, from which they would emerge only at a triumphant peace. The crumbling—not of their front trenches only but of their whole first position—was such a shock as King Priam's court must have received when the Wooden Horse disgorged the Greeks in the heart of their citadel.
>
> It was not won without stark fighting. The British soldiers were quick to kindle in the fight, and more formidable figures than those bronzed, steel-hatted warriors history has never seen on a field of battle. Those who witnessed the charge of the Highlanders at Loos were not likely to forget its fierce resolution. Said a French officer who was present: " I don't know what effect it had on the Boche, but it made *my* blood run cold." Our men were fighting against the foes of humanity, and they did not make war as a joke. But there was none of the savagery which comes either from a half-witted militarism or from rattled nerves. The Ger-

Propaganda in action. Here's an extract from John Buchan's History of the War Vol 16, The Battle of the Somme, *describing the battle's first day on 1 July 1916. Published just months later, and sold in vast numbers, this quasi-history earned Buchan a lot of money.*

2. BLOOD MILL

Many generals still dreamed of the great breakthrough battle. It was, they figured, just a matter of concentrating enough men, guns, and shells. Others resigned themselves to attrition – and made it the new military doctrine.

Field-Marshal Falkenhayn, the German commander on the Western Front, planned a 'blood mill' for 1916. He would launch a major offensive at Verdun, a fortress-city near the Franco-German border which, he argued, the French could not afford to lose.

> *The French General Staff would be compelled to throw in every man they have. If they do so, the forces of France will bleed to death – as there can be no question of voluntary withdrawal – whether we reach our goal or not ...*

The aim at Verdun was neither manoeuvre nor breakthrough: it was simply to kill. It lasted ten months and cost a million casualties. When the British attacked on the Somme that summer, it was in part to relieve the pressure on their French allies.

'At a steady pace'

Britain's regular army had been destroyed in 1914. Its territorial army was destroyed in 1915. Now it was the turn of the New Army of wartime citizen-soldiers.

Almost 2.5 million men had volunteered for Kitchener's New Army since the start of the war. Some had been swept up in the nationalist fervour of 1914. Some, seeking escape from humdrum lives of factory labour and slum housing, were lured by the prospect of travel, adventure, glory. Some decided to go because their mates were going. Some wanted to prove their manhood and patriotism.

The British Army of 1916 was several times larger than ever before. By early summer, a large proportion of it was massed in the Somme sector of the Western Front. The British were to attack north of the river, their French allies south of it.

The battle opened with a week-long bombardment by about 1,500 guns. This was designed to destroy the enemy's barbed-wire, smash his trenches, and take out his artillery. It did none of these things.

At zero hour on 1 July, the attackers went over the top. They should have raced across no-man's-land to reach the enemy trenches before the Germans could emerge from their dugouts and man their parapets.

But General Rawlinson, the British commander on the Somme, did not trust his soldiers. 'Neither our new formations nor the old divisions have the same discipline that obtained in our army a year ago,' he claimed. He feared the new working-class volunteers would go to ground and stay put. So they were to be kept on a tight leash. 'The assaulting troops must forward at a steady pace in successive lines ...'

The German machine-gunners won the race to the parapet on the Somme because of the class character of the British Army in 1916. It was a bourgeois army fighting an imperialist war in which upper-class generals distrusted the 'workers in uniform' under their command.

New tactics of 'fire and movement' and 'infiltration' were already widely practised. But they required devolved command and local initiative. Rawlinson was old school.

Let the fate of the 31st Division stand testimony for the rest. It was formed of pals' battalions from Accrington, Barnsley, Bradford, Durham, Halifax, Hull, Leeds, and Sheffield: mill workers, metal workers, miners.

As the whistles blew and they went over, they were hit by a wall of exploding shells and sheets of machine-gun fire. Hundreds were down within minutes.

Formations fell apart and little groups of men huddled in shell-holes. Some tried to get forwards but found the German wire impenetrable. The handfuls who reached the enemy line were soon hunted down and destroyed. By the end of the day, the 31st Division had suffered 3,600 casualties, and made no gains at all.

'A muddy grave'?

The first day of the Somme was a catastrophe. Though made worse by the stupidity of the British officer class, this is only part of the story. On some parts of the line, more intelligent tactics were employed, and as time went on, more officers adopted these.

As well as better tactics, there were new weapons. Tanks spearheaded a fresh assault on the Somme in September, their first appearance in war.

But this did not reduce the casualties. As tactics changed on one side, they also changed on the other. When one army acquired a new weapon, the opposing army devised a response. A rising mass of men and machines, a growing sophistication in the waging of war, merely intensified the 'war of attrition'.

Douglas Haig, the overall British commander on the Western Front, had hoped for a decisive breakthrough on the Somme. He continued his attacks for almost five months in the hope of achieving this.

In practice, the Somme, like Verdun, was only ever an attritional battle, and in consequence Haig followed the logic of attrition, even demanding higher casualty returns as a measure of British effort. 'The total losses of this division are under a thousand,' he complained of the 49th Division after one attack in September 1916.

He chose to avoid contact with casualties. It was his duty, he explained, *not* to visit front-line medical posts 'because these visits made him physically ill'. He relied instead on the reports of subordinates. 'The spirit of the wounded was beyond all praise,' he reported of a conversation with a military surgeon. 'All are now very confident, very cheery, and full of pluck. Truly the British race is the finest on Earth!'

Trench satirists loved to mock the pompous guff of Daily Mail journalist William Beach Thomas. Here, 'Teech Bomas' writes in The Somme Times, 31 July 1916.

HOW THE TANKS WENT OVER.
—:o:—
BY OUR SPECIAL CORRESPONDENT, Mr. TEECH BOMAS.
—:o:—

In the grey and purple light of a September morn they went over. Like great prehistoric monsters they leapt and skipped with joy when the signal came. It was my great good fortune to be a passenger on one of them How can I clearly relate what happened ? All is one chaotic mingling of joy and noise No fear ! How could one fear anything in the belly of a perambulating peripatetic progolódymythorus. Wonderful, epic, on we went, whilst twice a minute the 17in. gun on the roof barked out its message of defiance. At last we were fairly in amongst the Huns. They were round us in millions and in millions they died. Every wag of our creatures tail threw a bomb with deadly precision, and the mad, muddled, murderers melted. How describe the joy with which our men joined the procession until at last we had a train ten miles long. Our creature then became in festive mood and, jumping two villages, came to rest in a crump-hole. After surveying the surrounding country from there we started rounding up the prisoners. Then with a wag of our tail (which accounted for 20 Huns) and some flaps with our fins on we went. With a triumphant snort we went through Bapaume pushing over the church in a playful moment and then steering a course for home, feeling that our perspiring panting proglodomyte had thoroughly enjoyed its run over the disgruntled, discomfited, disembowelled earth. And so to rest in its lair ready for the morrow and what that morrow might hold. I must get back to the battle   TEECH BOMAS.

Revisionist historians see virtue in Haig's commitment to attrition. For Oxford historian Hew Strachan,

> *...the Somme could be seen as a waypoint on the route to winning the war in 1918 ... many senior officers had begun to conclude that, given the difficulty of achieving a breakthrough, the aim of an offensive should not be defined territorially but economically. The answer was to force the enemy to fight so as to exhaust his reserves ...*

On this basis, the Somme can be seen as some sort of 'victory' because the Germans suffered more heavily than the British. 'The year 1916 can only be fairly judged,' writes military historian Gary Sheffield,

> *...if one sees it in the context of the whole war, for the attrition inflicted on the Germans on the Somme and in subsequent battles made possible the victory of 1918. In this view, the Somme was the 'muddy grave' of the Imperial German Army.*

A further refinement is to laud the Somme as the battle in which the British Army learned the art of modern war. 'The five-month Somme battle, says Paddy Griffith,

> *...taught the BEF [the British Expeditionary Force] many lessons and transformed it from a largely inexperienced mass army into a largely experienced one ... Despite the deep attrition that was unquestionably gnawing its destructive path through units which had been in the line since 1914-15, the Somme battle actually left the majority of healthy survivors in surprisingly good shape.*

None of this is convincing. There are no good grounds for saying that the damage to the German Army on the Somme was greater than that to the British. The German Army continued to fight – against the odds – until October 1918. Before then, in 1917, it was the *French Army* that mutinied, and the *Russian Army* that made revolution.

Nor was Britain immune to a rising tide of anti-war sentiment. The flow of volunteers dried up and conscription had to be introduced. But some 200,000 people signed an anti-conscription petition, and within six months, three-quarters of a million men had appealed against their call-up.

Harry Patch, the last British veteran of the trenches (he died in 2009), had just turned 18 when his call-up telegram arrived in October 1916.

> *I didn't want to join up ... I didn't want to go and fight anyone ... army life didn't appeal to me at all ... I mean, why should I go out and kill somebody I never knew, and for what reason? I wasn't at all patriotic.*

Conscription was unpopular, and so was exploitation by capitalists and landlords on the home front. In the winter of 1915/16, tenants on Glasgow estates went on rent strike and were supported by strikes in the Clydeside shipyards and engineering factories.

More and bigger strikes followed: some 200,000 workers were out across northern Britain in the spring of 1917. An estimated 2.6 million British workers were involved in industrial action during the First World War, and union membership increased from 4.1 to 6.5 million. The war was radicalising the British working class. The Army was also infected. Behind the jingoism of politicians and press lies a hidden history of mutiny. The biggest was probably that at the brutal 'Bull Ring' training facility at Étaples in northern France in September 1917, when thousands of men refused to obey orders, attacked the hated

'Red Cap' military police, and broke out of the camp and ran amok in the neighbouring town.

There was nothing inevitable about the fact that the German Army buckled first on the Western Front. The popular revolt against the war and the system that had caused it was global.

A rash of popular songs supported official efforts to recruit the manpower needed for the First World War. Female stars of the music hall vied to shame men into joining up. There were few anti-war voices in popular entertainment, though in 1915 I Didn't Raise My Boy to be a Soldier *became a surprise hit in the United States, selling 650,000 copies in its first year. Songs like this would seldom be sung on British stages, even though mass strikes were demonstrating the depth of discontent with the war.*

3. A WAR FOR EMPIRE AND PROFIT

Revisionist historians operate in a bubble-world of their own making. They study government papers and military documents, and piece together the details of high-level scheming and strategy.

But the bubble-world of statesmen and generals is carried along in history's great river. To explain the past, we must see the river.

Revisionists argue that the First World War had to be fought because Germany was aggressive and militaristic, a 'rogue state' that threatened 'the balance of power' and 'the peace of Europe'. Germany's leaders, they warn, were increasing their army and fleet, had plans to wage an offensive war, and aimed to create a German-dominated continental empire.

But it is equally true that some German leaders were more cautious, doubting Germany's ability to win, seeking to avoid war at the outset, and later making overtures for peace – which were rejected by Britain, France, and Russia.

Germany's rulers were, in fact, divided. It is not difficult to fathom why. The central issue was how to respond to the threat posed by the British Empire.

The British controlled the biggest empire in the world. And the idea that 'democratic' empires like the British were somehow preferable to 'autocratic' ones like the German – as historian Niall Ferguson has argued – is myopic. Only half of working-class men had the vote in Britain, and no women of any class. There was nothing remotely 'democratic' about British rule in Egypt or India. There was certainly nothing 'democratic' about the artillery and machine-guns used to massacre the Sudanese at Omdurman.

The British could match the Germans atrocity for atrocity. While the Germans were exterminating the Herero people of Namibia, for example, the British in neighbouring South Africa were machine-gunning Zulu farmers to enforce a poll tax designed to drive them off the land and into the gold mines – that is, they were inventing the apartheid system.

Anglo-German rivalry

In the years before 1914, Britain's rulers, while feigning injured innocence, pursued a provocatively anti-German policy. They formed alliances with France and Russia to encircle Germany and threaten her rulers with the war on two fronts they so feared.

It was this that forced German military leaders to plan for a pre-emptive strike against France as soon as war was declared, allowing their enemies to cast them as 'aggressors'.

The British also began building huge new 'dreadnought' battleships, quickly outpacing Germany in a naval arms race. They soon had the bulk of their fleet concentrated in the North Sea, where it threatened Germany with blockade.

Pre-war British diplomacy aimed at preventing German colonial expansion in North Africa and Latin America, and shutting German business out of other foreign markets.

The British, moreover, had expansionist plans of their own in 1914. They made a secret agreement with the French and the Russians to partition the Ottoman Empire in 1916. And when the war ended, Britain's share of the global carve-up negotiated at Versailles included Iraq, Jordan, Palestine, Cameroun, Togoland, and Tanzania.

As a result of the First World War, the British Empire was larger in the 1920s than ever before, having gained a further 1.8 million square miles of territory and 13 million new subjects.

Anglo-German rivalry had fuelled the drive to war. Other great powers had also clashed increasingly over borders, colonies, and commercial opportunities.

Why had geopolitical competition between states reached such intensity by the early 20th century that it led to an arms race and world war? There had been no major European war since 1815. What had changed in the run-up to 1914?

A systemic crisis

The First World War was the culmination of rising imperialist tension. As the European economy expanded – swelling the fortunes of the rich to unprecedented levels – the giant industrial corporations within each nation-state competed for raw materials, markets, and investment opportunities abroad. They were funded by powerful banking syndicates. And they were supported by the armies and navies of the great powers.

Profit, empire, and armaments were meshed together. The Russian revolutionary Nikolai Bukharin put it thus:

> *When competition has finally reached its highest stage, when it has become competition between state-capitalist trusts, then the use of state power, and the possibilities connected with it, begins to play a very large part ... The more strained the situation in the world sphere of struggle – and our epoch is characterised by the greatest intensity of competition between 'national' groups of finance capital – the more often an appeal is made to the mailed fist of state power.*

Economic competition between banks and industrial conglomerates had fused with geopolitical competition between states. The world had divided into militarised national-capitalist blocs. It was this that produced the titanic confrontation of the First World War – a war of unprecedented ferocity, global in scope, industrial in scale.

Left to themselves, the rulers of the world would have prevented peace until one of what Bukharin called 'the national groups of finance capital' had smashed the other and was thus able to re-divide the world in its own interest. Until then, the war – the waste, the killing, the suffering, the insanity – would simply increase.

Accidents of history and geography determined the stances of the great powers. Germany was a continental power recently unified and fast-developing. Britain was an island with an established overseas empire, and, crucially, an economy beginning to lag behind its competitors.

In the middle of the 19th century, Britain had produced half the world's iron and steel. By the mid-1890s, Britain produced less iron and steel than either Germany or the US. The gap between Britain and her commercial rivals was even greater in new industries like chemicals and electro-technics.

The British had always been prepared to intervene aggressively in Europe to prevent any one power dominating the continent. It had been consistent British policy to maintain Europe as 'a continent of warring states'. That had been the reason for Britain's war against Philip II of Spain in the late 16th century, against Louis XIV of France in the early 18th century, and against Napoleon in the early 19th century.

That traditional policy was the reason for the war against the Kaiser in 1914 – though now linked with a new determination to beat back competition from German capitalists and keep them locked out of foreign markets.

Like US leaders today, British leaders a century ago used military power to shore up a weakening economy.

From factory-fresh to spent upon the field, huge volumes of munitions and supplies were demanded by the First World War. These boosted the fortunes of industrialists within each participating nation.

From war to revolution

Few at first saw through the patriotic fervour of 1914. The opponents of war were a small minority of socialists, trade unionists, and pacifists. The men who fought on the Somme – the volunteer soldiers of Kitchener's New Army – were the victims of a wave of jingoism and militarism that reached into all corners of British society.

But by 1916 – and especially after the Somme – mounting casualties and privation were producing mutinies, strikes, and protests. From 1917 onwards, a wave of revolt from below, opposing both war and the system that spawned it, swept across Europe.

Eventually, there were revolutions in Russia, Germany, Austria, and Hungary, and mass strikes and demonstrations in Britain, France, and Italy.

In Russia and Germany, in particular, it was ordinary soldiers, sailors, and workers who finally brought the slaughter to an end.

When Russian soldiers – most of them conscripted peasants – joined crowds of revolutionary workers on the streets of Petrograd in February 1917, the 300-year-old dynasty of the Romanovs collapsed.

The same soldiers supported a second revolution, in October 1917, after the new Provisional Government had continued the war. As a letter signed by 25 front-line soldiers explained:

> *We have been very sad to read bourgeois newspapers ... which assure us that we need war to a victorious conclusion, that we need an offensive to win back the land seized by the enemy. Haven't the bourgeoisie and the capitalists already filled their pockets with bloody coins? We workers and peasants, dressed in our grey overcoats, do not need this bloody slaughter. Enough of decimating peoples! We don't need conquests! We need peace – peace for all mankind.*

When German sailors – most of them conscripted workers – refused to put to sea and arrested their officers in October 1918, they triggered a revolution which ended the rule of Prussia's even more ancient Hohenzollern dynasty.

They, too, had turned against the war. As one revolutionary sailor told a German admiral in Kiel, the naval base on the north German coast:

> *We sailors have grown very tired of the long war. We want peace. Unfortunately the officers did not share this feeling ... Fearing that an attack was about to take place, when the fleet was ordered to sail out, the crews refused to obey orders ...*

In Britain, at the same time, the Armistice left many veterans of the Somme cold. Sassoon found the streets of London clogged with people cheering and waving flags. It was, he wrote, 'a loathsome ending to the loathsome tragedy of the last four years'.

The answer came the following year. The storm of discontent accumulating through the long years of war exploded in 1919. A wave of strikes and demonstrations swept the country and brought it to the brink of revolution. Miners, railwaymen, and transport workers formed a 'triple alliance'. Shipyards and engineering factories joined the action. Militants on the Clyde called for a general strike. Even the police went on strike that year.

One Labour MP referred to 'the industrial unrest and social discontent that is seething like a mad whirlpool around us'. He felt that the smallest action might prove to be 'a match applied to a powder magazine'.

The industrial unrest at home coincided with a wave of revolt across the Empire. A nationalist insurgency overwhelmed British security forces in Ireland. An anti-colonial revolt erupted against British rule in Egypt. The Indian independence movement surged following a massacre of unarmed demonstrators.

Sometimes mutinous British soldiers made common cause with anti-colonial rebels. When men ordered to break a strike by Egyptian railworkers in 1919 refused, their commanding general was powerless, complaining,

> Some trade union microbe has got into them ... I can't shoot them all for mutiny ... one reason given by the men was that to work on the railway would be 'strike-breaking'.

The rulers of the world – warmongers, imperialists, profiteers – faced a mighty revolt of the people of the world between 1917 and 1921 that perhaps came closer to ending the system responsible for war than at any time in history. Its ultimate failure is replete with tragedy. For, in consequence, in the next generation, the world would have to face the barbarism of Auschwitz and Hiroshima.

Revisionist historians like Max Hastings – defenders of a system that endlessly produces such horrors, from the Somme to Stalingrad to Vietnam to Iraq – castigate the middle-class 'whingeing' of the war-poets. Socialists and pacifists, by contrast, celebrate their art, since they share the revulsion at war and the hostility to warmongers.

So let us give the final word to Sassoon, a veteran of the Somme, who, in his poem 'Aftermath', testifies to the true meaning of the battle. 'Have you forgotten yet?' he asks.

> *Do you remember the rats, and the stench of corpses rotting in front of the front-line trench, and dawn coming, dirty-white, and chill with a hopeless rain? Do you ever stop and ask, 'Is it all going to happen again?'*

DANDELIONS

Steve O'Donoghue

Now Arthur was only a young cub
A brave lion and merely fifteen
But with the rest of his pack, he was sent to attack
To a war that was cruel and obscene.

But those lions fought hard and fought bravely
While the donkeys just grazed in a field
They had no sense of shame for their barbarous game
And the thousands of lions they killed.

> *And when he saw them marching up Whitehall*
> *I remember what old Arthur said*
> *He said 'The donkeys are all wearing poppies*
> *So I shall wear dandelions instead.'*

Now every Remembrance Sunday
Well I pause at eleven o'clock
And I remember those dandy young lions
And those donkeys and their poppycock,

Cos they've taken those beautiful poppies
And they use them to glorify war.
Well I remember those dandy young lions
And I don't wear a poppy no more.

> *And when he saw them marching up Whitehall*
> *I remember what old Arthur said*

He's hanging on the old barbed wire

> He said 'The donkeys are all wearing poppies
> So I shall wear dandelions instead.'

'Now if you take an old dandelion
And just blow it quite gently,' he'd say
'You can see all the dreams of those soldiers
In the seeds as they just float away.'

But then the wind takes hold of those seeds
And they rise and quickly they soar,
Like the spirit of all those old soldiers
Who believed that their war would end war.

> 'Cos those lions were dandy young workers
> Who those donkeys so cruelly misled
> And if the donkeys are gonna wear poppies
> I shall wear dandelions instead.'

Steve O'Donoghue explains, 'Most of the song is true, though I have used some artistic license. Arthur was my maternal grandfather. He joined up as a boy, lying about his age, as lots of kids did. He was a sort of yellow colour due to the mustard gas. He never talked about the war other than to say, "I've seen things no man should have to see" and "they promised us homes fit for heroes and we got heroes fit for homes". He was not necessarily anti-poppies but was very anti-war. He hated Churchill with a vengeance, thinking him a "war-mongering bastard". He was a leading shopfloor rep in the print union and would talk at length about the general strike and politics, but not the war. All the dandelion and Whitehall stuff is just poetic license, but I would like to think it represents his views.'

HARRY PATCH

Harry Patch, who died aged 111 in 2009, was one of the last surviving soldiers known to have fought in the First World War. Patch refused to talk about the war until 1998. Thence, as a centenarian, he became one of the clearest voices to declare there is no glory in war.

'Politicians who took us to war should have been given the guns and told to settle their differences themselves, instead of organising nothing better than legalised mass murder.'

'We weren't heroes. We didn't want to be there. We were scared. We all were, all the time. And any man who tells you he wasn't is a damn liar.' 2007.

On coming face to face with a German soldier, 'I had about five seconds to make the decision. I brought him down, but I didn't kill him ... any one of them could have been me.' 2007.

On meeting a German veteran aged 107 in 2004, 'Once, to have shaken the hand of the enemy would have been treason, but Charles and I agreed on so much about that awful war. A nice old chap, he was. Why he should have been my enemy, I don't know.'

On revisiting Passchendaele in 2007, he said war is 'the calculated and condoned slaughter of human beings.'

When Tony Blair posed with him for a photo in 2006, Patch said, 'War is organised murder.' Blair did not linger.